THE BULLY-FREE ZONE

ARE YOU BEING BULLIED?

THERESE HARASYMIW

PowerKiDS
press

New York

Published in 2021 by The Rosen Publishing Group, Inc.
29 East 21st Street, New York, NY 10010

First Edition

Portions of this work were originally authored by Addy Ferguson and published as *What to Do If You Are Bullied*. All new material in this edition authored by Therese Harasymiw.

Editor: Therese Harasymiw
Book Design: Reann Nye

Photo Credits: Cover, p. 6 Africa Studio/Shutterstock.com; series art Here/Shutterstock.com; p. 5 pathdoc/Shutterstock.com; p. 5 Lopolo/Shutterstock.com; p. 7 myboys.me/Shutterstock.com; p. 9 Peter Dazeley/The Image Bank/Getty Images; p. 11 Syda Productions/Shutterstock.com; p. 12 Motortion Films/Shutterstock.com; p. 13 wavebreakmedia/Shutterstock.com; p. 15 Motortion/iStock/Getty Images Plus/Getty Images; p. 17 SDI Productions/E+/Getty Images; p. 18 JGI/Jamie Grill/Getty Images; p. 19 MoMo Productions/ DigitalVision/Getty Images; p. 21 Tim Pannell/Getty Images; p. 22 Stephanie Rausser/Stone/Getty Images.

Some of the images in this book illustrate individuals who are models. The depictions do not imply actual situations or events.

Library of Congress Cataloging-in-Publication Data

Names: Harasymiw, Therese, author.
Title: Are you being bullied? / Therese Harasymiw.
Description: New York : PowerKids Press, 2020. | Series: The bully-free zone | Includes index.
Identifiers: LCCN 2019059445 | ISBN 9781725319561 (paperback) | ISBN 9781725319585 (library binding) | ISBN 9781725319578 (6 pack)
Subjects: LCSH: Bullying–Juvenile literature. | Bullying in schools–Juvenile literature. | Bullying–Prevention–Juvenile literature.
Classification: LCC BF637.B85 H353 2020 | DDC 302.34/3–dc23
LC record available at https://lccn.loc.gov/2019059445

Manufactured in the United States of America

CPSIA Compliance Information: Batch #CSPK20. For Further Information contact Rosen Publishing, New York, New York at 1-800-237-9932.

Find us on

CONTENTS

ARE YOU A BULLYING VICTIM?

Have you ever been picked on or teased by classmates in the lunchroom or playground? Have you been bumped or pushed in the halls on purpose? If this **behavior** happens more than once, it's called bullying. The people who **taunt** or hurt others are called bullies.

Bullying happens a lot in schools. This doesn't mean it shouldn't be stopped. And it's not just a part of growing up. Bullying is never okay. Each of us has the power to stand up to the people who bully us. Bullying can be stopped. Are you ready to take on bullying?

IN THE ZONE

The website Stopbullying.gov says a mean or hurtful behavior that's likely to happen again is bullying. It doesn't even have to happen many times.

Bullies are more powerful than their victims in some way. They might be stronger or more popular.

MANY FORMS OF BULLYING

Did you know there's more than one kind of bullying? Some is physical, which means it has to do with the body. It takes the form of pushing, hitting, hurting, or trying to **injure** someone. This kind of bullying is easy to **identify**.

Cyberbullies use computers, smartphones, online games, and tablets to harm others.

Verbal bullying has to do with harmful words. It's calling people names, teasing them, scaring them, or telling lies about them. Cyberbullying is bullying that happens on the internet or through text messages. Bullies can also hurt others by **ignoring** or leaving them out. This is called social bullying. Have any of these kinds of bullying happened to you?

WHY DO PEOPLE BULLY?

If you have been bullied, you might wonder why someone would hurt you like that. It's often not about you. Some bullies treat others badly because they have low self-esteem, which means they don't feel good about themselves. Some have parents or other family members who are bullies. Some bullies don't have **empathy** toward others. They may believe bullying makes them popular too.

No matter the reasons, bullying is wrong. Parents, teachers, principals, and others have been working to educate young people about bullying. They're telling people what to look for so bullying can be identified. They're also sharing effective ways of stopping bullying.

Bullying isn't always out in the open. It's hard to spot cyberbullying, for example, unless you're the victim.

BULLYING HURTS

Bullying can have real and lasting effects. If you've been bullied, you may feel hopeless, scared, **embarrassed**, angry, and alone. All of these feelings are common.

You may not want to go to school because you don't want to see the bully. Your grades may drop if you miss school. You may have a hard time studying and paying attention in class too.

Bullying can cause low self-esteem, **depression**, and **anxiety**. If it's allowed to go on for a long time, some victims go to great lengths to stop the pain, even hurting themselves or others.

WARNING SIGNS OF BULLYING

- injuries
- lost or broken belongings
- real or pretend health problems, such as headaches
- changes in eating patterns
- having a hard time sleeping

- missing school and dropping grades
- staying away from friends and social events
- low self-esteem
- self-harm

Sometimes, people don't tell others they're being bullied. Look for the common warning signs that someone is a victim of bullying.

DON'T REACT

If you're being bullied, you might feel like there's nothing you can do. There are a few things to try though.

Most bullies are looking for a **reaction**. They want to make someone upset, scared, or even angry. They want to use these feelings against the victim. If you can, you could try looking your bully in the eyes and telling them to leave you alone. Then, walk away. If the bully doesn't get a reaction, they may leave you alone. If it doesn't work, tell an adult.

12

IN THE ZONE

Some people suggest looking at the bully and replying with a joke. Then, walk away. That can be hard if you're feeling scared or angry though.

Staying calm after being bullied is really hard. If you don't think you can, just walk away without speaking.

If you're a victim of cyberbullying, you should always ignore the bully. Tell an adult right away.

DON'T FIGHT

If you're dealing with a physical bully, it may seem like the best **defense** is to fight back. Just as bullying is wrong, fighting is wrong. Even if the bully started the fight, you could get in trouble if you continue it. You're also likely to get hurt. You could even hurt the bully, and hurting another person is never the answer. In fact, you might be called a bully!

If a bully is trying to fight you and you cannot get away, call for help. Send a friend or classmate to find an adult. Bullies want attention, but not from adults.

IN THE ZONE

There's a difference between telling and tattling on a bully. Tattling is to get someone in trouble. Telling is to **protect** yourself and others.

Bystanders, or people who watch bullying, can help. They can get an adult to stop it. They can also offer support to the victim.

ADULTS CAN HELP

According to a study of U.S. schools, less than half of all kids who are bullied tell an adult. They may be afraid that telling will make the bully angry. They may be embarrassed. They may think that adults around them don't care or won't help them.

Talking to a trusted adult, such as a parent or teacher, is important. These adults can help you figure out a way to stop the bullying. Even more important, they can form a plan to make school a safer place for everyone. It truly takes a community to stop bullying.

Bullied kids say the most important thing adults can do is listen and give advice.

DEALING WITH FEELINGS

The bad feelings that come from being bullied can continue long after the bullying stops. If you've been bullied, your most important job is building your self-esteem back up. Sometimes, you need a bit of help to do that.

IN THE ZONE

Bullies often end up in trouble. However, bullies can learn to change their behavior.

18

Building new friendships is an effective way of fighting low self-esteem.

School counselors are people who are trained to listen and help you in many ways. They'll also teach you effective ways to deal with a bully that you'll be comfortable with. In addition, they can suggest ways to boost your self-esteem. For example, taking part in clubs and teams can make you feel good as well as rebuild your self-esteem.

EMPATHY FOR ALL

One bully may stop because they get in enough trouble or realize what they're doing is wrong. However, it takes a school community working together to stop bullying overall. The most successful anti-bullying programs are those that teach empathy and respect.

When kids have empathy for each other, they're much less likely to bully. They're also much more likely to stick up for those who are being bullied. They realize they should do this even for those they don't know or aren't friends with. This takes bravery, but it feels good to know you're doing the right thing!

IN THE ZONE

Anti-bullying programs in schools should continue through the year. Just one talk or a single day of learning about bullying isn't enough.

Empathy is about making connections. It's about understanding how others are feeling because you feel that way sometimes too.

21

TAKING ACTION

It's important to remember that being bullied isn't your fault. You didn't cause it. No one deserves to be bullied.

If you have been bullied, another way to feel better is to take action against future bullying. Talk to your school counselor or principal about starting a "no-bullying" program at your school. You can help other victims of bullying. You may even convince bullies to give up the behavior. Most important, if you see bullying happen to someone around you, stand up and speak out. If everyone did that, we might stop bullying in its tracks.

GLOSSARY

anxiety: Strong fear or worry about what will happen.

behavior: A way of acting.

defense: Something used to protect or guard yourself from harm.

depression: A medical condition in which one feels sad, hopeless, or unimportant much of the time.

embarrass: To cause somebody to be ashamed or ill at ease.

empathy: The feeling that one understands and shares in another person's experiences and emotions.

identify: To know or find out who or what something is.

ignore: To do nothing about or in response to something. Also, to pretend not to notice.

injure: To harm or damage someone or something.

protect: To keep something or someone from being harmed.

reaction: The way someone acts or feels in response to something that happens.

taunt: To insult someone to make them angry.

INDEX

WEBSITES

Due to the changing nature of Internet links, PowerKids Press has developed an online list of websites related to the subject of this book. This site is updated regularly. Please use this link to access the list: www.powerkidslinks.com/bullyfree/beingbullied

24